Achieving Institutional Exce

Sameer Aljamal

Achieving Institutional Excellence Through Many Variables

LAP LAMBERT Academic Publishing

Publisher:
LAP LAMBERT Academic Publishing
is a trademark of
International Book Market Service Ltd., member of OmniScriptum Publishing Group
17 Meldrum Street, Beau Bassin 71504, Mauritius

Printed at: see last page
ISBN: 978-613-9-95507-7

Table of Content

Achieving Institutional excellence through Organizational Justice and Transformational Management.

Prepared by: Dr. Sameer .S.Aljamal.
Email: sameeraljamal@yahoo.com
Mobile:00972569820506

Abstract:

The study aimed to identify the role of organizational justice and transformational management in achieving institutional excellence from the point of view of workers in the directorates of education in Hebron, according to the variables (gender, age, scientific qualification, job title, years of service, and Directorate). The study followed the descriptive analytical approach. The study sample consisted of (103) employees by (10.3%) of the total size of the society. The researcher used a questionnaire consisting of (98) paragraphs: (33) paragraphs for measuring organizational justice, (41) paragraphs for measuring transformational management, and (24) paragraphs for measuring institutional excellence. The results indicated that the level of organizational justice, and the level of transformational management, and the level of institutional excellence in the directorates of education in Hebron is medium in general. The fields of regulatory justice were respectively: (interactive justice, distributive justice, evaluative justice, procedural justice). The results showed that there are no statistically significant differences in the degree of organizational justice and its role in achieving institutional excellence according to the variables (age, academic qualification, job title, directorate). While there were differences of statistical significance in the degree of organizational justice and its role in achieving institutional excellence according to variables(gender, years of service). The differences were in favor of workers whose service is less than 5 years. The study revealed a significant and significant correlation between organizational justice and institutional excellence. The fields of regulatory transformational management were respectively: (thought-provoking, inspirational motivation, ideal influence, individual interest). The fields of regulatory institutional were respectively:(leadership excellence, excellence in service delivery, human excellence).

The results showed that there are no statistically significant differences in the degree of practice of transformational management and its role in achieving institutional excellence from the point of view of workers in the directorates of education in Hebron governorate due to the variables: scientific qualification, age, years of service and Directorate), While differences were found to be statistically significant by gender variable and the differences were in favor of males. There is a statistically significant correlation between the practice of transformational management and the achievement of institutional excellence from the point of view of workers in the directorates of education in Hebron on the overall degree, and in all areas of transformational management (ideal effect, inspirational motivation, thought provoking, individual consideration).

The study came out with several recommendations: (The Palestinian Ministry of Education and Higher Education should amend the prevailing procedures and laws in order to raise the level of organizational justice because of its active role in achieving institutional excellence, Work on the development of an effective system of incentives and granting appropriate financial incentives for workers to achieve the desired institutional excellence, Amend the civil service law to suit the needs of employees and achieve the public interest, The need to reward outstanding employees in performance (positive motivation), Holding training courses for employees and informing them of the latest developments in the field of administrative sciences and the mechanism of achieving competitive advantage in the institution, and work to send distinguished employees, The Ministry of Education should reduce the centralization of the work, Work to improve the functional conditions of administrative staff, Non-concentration of powers in the hands of the official and encourage the delegation of powers to subordinates, Urge officials to deal satisfactorily with employees, Urge officials to raise the challenge and consistency of employees, The need to provide an atmosphere of trust and security between the president and the subordinate, Provide rewards for employees to suit their evaluation, Providing scholarships for distinguished employees.

Key words: *Organizational Justice, Transformational Management, institutional Excellence*

Introduction:

The success or failure of institutions to the success achieved by administrative leaders in their businesses, through the performance of roles and functions entrusted to them, and their contribution to the development of their organizations, according to their abilities and aptitudes enabling them to influence others to achieve their goals (Taweel, 1999).

Transformational management as described by Burns is the process through which seeks both Commander and subordinates to advance each, in order to reach higher levels of motivation and morality, and transforming subordinates to leaders, and leaders to moral codes (Owens, 1995).

Organizational justice is a regulatory phenomenon and a relative concept, because of the impact that workers' sense of justice or injustice can have on the workplace. Which can lead to a decline in the levels of organizational performance no matter how strong the other components of the administrative process, one of the important organizational variables affecting the efficiency of the performance of employees on the one hand and the performance of the organization on the other in cases where the workers' Such as low job satisfaction, low organizational citizenship behaviors, low organizational commitment, and generally low overall job performance. In contrast, the increased sense of justice leads to increased confidence in the management of the organization, increased conviction of access to rights and the consequent elevation of individual behavior after reassurance of justice and trust in the organization. (Zayed, 2006).

Sociologists have long been alerted to the importance of the principles of justice and their values provided by Islam primarily for the outstanding performance of the organizations and for the satisfaction of the individuals working in them, which prompted the modern administration to focus their attention on many phenomena related to the concept of justice as employment choices and equal pay " To consider organizational justice as one of the basic components of the social and psychological structure of the organization (Miles, 2000), where organizational justice is a "social value and social pattern, whose absence poses serious risks to both the institution and the individual. Justice leads them to negative behavioral practices, such as lack of loyalty to the organization and intention to leave, increase turnover, as well as reprisals towards the institution or its leaders. Organizational justice is intrinsically linked to the values of workers and their social relationships, and they directly affect the motivations and efforts of workers, which has led to one of the most important theories of human behavior in organizations for a long time. (Zayed, 2006).

The concern for organizational justice is due to several reasons, notably: the need to abandon destructive bureaucratic regulatory policies, the feelings of injustice and threats of workers, and to adopt other ethical policies of organizational justice and organizational support to ensure long-term organizational continuity and effectiveness. There is a challenge in seeking to reduce or prevent the anti-social behavior of staff resulting mainly from the lack of regulatory justice. (Awad, 2003).

Study problem and questions:
I've turned the role of managers of the supervisory role to a facilitator, creating a shared vision and inclusive organization and encourages participation in decision making, and cooperation among members of the organization which reflects on their sense of responsibility. Where studies have shown that there is a relationship between the characteristics of a learning organization and the innovation and excellence. Where excellence can be achieved without the employed within the enterprise content and integrated within their business. Although the concepts of equity and justice are among the most common concepts of the value structure of government administration, the interest of Western studies and research on organizational justice has been largely focused on the private sector, with less attention in the government sector (Adam, 2003), and therefore the employee's sense of equity and equality within the workplace enhances his or her affiliation with the institution and increases his or her professional satisfaction, which is reflected positively on performance, which leads to integration into the work and institutional excellence cannot be achieved without employees within the institution satisfied with their work And integrated into their work, and therefore can identify the problem of the study by answering the following questions:

The main question1:
What is the degree of organizational justice and its role in achieving institutional excellence from the point of view of workers in the directorates of education in Hebron ?, and the following sub-questions arise from it:
Q1) What is the degree of organizational justice in the directorates of education in Hebron from the point of view of its employees?
Q2) What is the degree of procedural justice in the directorates of education in Hebron from the point of view of its employees?
Q3) What is the degree of distributive justice in the directorates of education in Hebron from the point of view of its employees?
Q4) What is the degree of interactive justice in the directorates of education in the governorate of Hebron from the point of view of its employees?
Q5) What is the degree of evaluation justice in the directorates of education in Hebron from the point of view of its employees?
Q6) What is the degree of institutional excellence in the directorates of education in the governorate of Hebron from the point of view of its employees?
Q7) What is the degree of leadership excellence in the directorates of education in the province of Hebron from the point of view of its employees?
Q8) What is the degree of human excellence in the directorates of education in Hebron from the point of view of its employees?
Q9) What is the degree of excellence in providing service in the directorates of education in the province of Hebron from the point of view of its employees?
Q10) Is there a correlation between the degree of organizational justice and the achievement of institutional excellence in the directorates of education in Hebron from the point of view of its employees?
Q11) Are there significant differences at the level of ($\alpha \leq 0.05$) in the degree of organizational justice and achieve institutional excellence in the directorates of

education in the governorate of Hebron from the point of view of their employees according to:(gender, scientific qualification, job title, years of service, directorate)?

The Main question2:
what is the practice of transformational management and its role in achieving organizational excellence from the perspective of working in school districts in Hebron?, and the following sub-questions arise from it:
Q1). What is the degree of the practice of transformational management from the point of view of workers in the directorates of education in Hebron governorate?

The hypotheses of the study:
To answer the study questions, the researcher formulated the following hypotheses:

*There are no statistically significant differences at the level of significance ($\alpha \leq 0.05$) in the degree of organizational justice and its role in achieving institutional excellence in the directorates of education in Hebron from the point of view of its employees according to the variables: (gender, Age, scientific qualification, job title, years of service, Directorate).
*There is no statistically significant relationship at the level of significance($\alpha \leq 0.05$)in the degree of organizational justice and achievement of institutional excellence in the directorates of education in Hebron from the point of view of its employees.
*There are no statistically significant differences at the level of significance ($\alpha \leq 0.05$) in the degree of the practice of transformational management and its role in achieving institutional excellence from the point of view of its employees in Hebron according to the variables: (gender, Age, scientific qualification, job title, years of service, Directorate).
*There is no statistically significant relationship at the level of significance ($\alpha \leq 0.05$) in the degree of practicing transformational management and achieving institutional excellence in the directorates of education in Hebron from the point of view of its employees.

Study variables:

First: The topographic variables:
1.**Gender**, has two levels: (male, female).
2.**Age**, has four levels: (less than 30 years, from 30 - less than 40 years, from 40- less than 50 years, from 50 years and more).
3.Scientific qualification, has three levels: (Diploma and less, Bachelor, MA and more).
4.**Job title**, has three levels: (Administrative Officer, Educational Supervisor, Head of Department).
5.**Years of service**, has four levels: (less than 5 years, 5 - less than 10 years, 10 - less than 15 years, 15 years and over)
6. **Directorate**, has four levels: (North Hebron, Hebron, South Hebron, Yatta).

Second: Independent variable: There are two independent variables:
Independent var1:
The degree of organizational justice in the directorates of education in Hebron.
Independent var2:
The practice of transformational management in the directorates of education in Hebron.

Third: dependent variable: Achieving organizational excellence in the directorates of education in Hebron.

Objectives of the study:
This study aims to identify:
1.The degree of organizational justice in the directorates of education in Hebron from the point of view of its employees.
2.The degree of the practice of transformational management in the directorates of education in Hebron from the point of view of its employees.
3.The level of institutional excellence in the directorates of education in Hebron from the point of view of its employees.
4.The Extent of a relationship between organizational justice and institutional excellence.
5. The extent of the relationship between the practice of transformational management and achieving institutional excellence.
6. Identify the extent of differences between the responses of the members of the study on the degree of organizational justice and its role in achieving organizational excellence in the directorates of education in Hebron from the point of view of its employees according to the following variables: (gender, Age, scientific qualification, job title, years of experience, Directorate) .
7. Identify the extent of differences between the responses of the members of the study on the practice of transformational management and achieving institutional excellence in the directorates of education in Hebron from the point of view of its employees according to the following variables: (gender, Age, scientific qualification, job title, years of experience, Directorate) .
8. Make proposals and recommendations to decision-makers to develop appropriate mechanisms and strategies for achieving institutional excellence.

The importance of the study:
The importance of this study can be summarized as follows:
1.The results of this study may benefit officials in identifying the degree of organizational justice in the directorates of education, which helps in the development of solutions and strategies necessary to achieve organizational justice.
2.The results of this study indicate that the officials of the Palestinian Ministry of Education know the practice of transformational management in the directorates of education in Hebron governorate from the point of view of workers, which helps in the development of appropriate plans, strategies and training programs.
3.Recognize the level of organizational excellence in the directorates of education, and come up with the recommendations necessary to reach a high level of institutional excellence.

Limitations of the study:
Limits of this study are as follows:
-Objective Limits:
The study deals with the degree of organizational justice and the practice of transformational management and their roles in achieving institutional excellence from the point of view of its employees.
-Human Limits:

The study is limited to employees working in the directorates of education in Hebron, with the exception of the Director of Education and his two deputies who are on their job until (30-6-2017).

-Time Limits:
The study is conducted during the months of July and August/ 2017.

-Spatial Limits:
Directorates of Education in Hebron.

Study terms:
The researcher will define the terms in the study according to the definitions in the Arabic and foreign references. Some terms will be defined according to the researcher's own experiences.

-Organizational Justice: (Adams, 1965), defined organizational justice as: equality, which involves an individual or employee comparing the rate of his output relative to his inputs with the rate of output of other colleagues relative to their inputs, where the rates are equal, justice is equal, and where the rates are not equal The individual then feels unjust.

-Procedural Justice: The researcher defines it as procedural: It is the employee's feeling of complete satisfaction with his inputs (his academic qualifications, his experience, his years of service, his efforts in work, etc.), and the outputs he receives as a result of doing his work.

-Distributive Justice: The researcher knows it procedurally as: the employee's sense of satisfaction with what he gets from the outputs of his work.

-Interactive justice: defined by the researcher procedural as: The employee feels that he is an integral part and important in the organization, and participate in the decisions that concern his work, treatment and non-discrimination in the sense of fairness of treatment and non-discrimination in the distribution of work.

-Evaluative justice: The researcher defines it procedurally as: processes, procedures and systems that guarantee the rights of employees, and that the evaluation of their performance levels is done in a fair and fair manner that achieves stability and job security.

-Institutional Excellence: "state of managerial innovation and organizational excellence achieves extraordinary high levels of performance and implementation of the production, marketing, financial and other processes in the organization, resulting in results and achievements that exceed what competitors achieve and are satisfied by customers and all stakeholders in the organization." (Selmi, 2001, p. 77).

-Human excellence: The researcher defines it procedurally as that workers who have a number of qualities that do not know them to be prominent and distinctive in one or several aspects.

-Service Excellence: All the internal activities and activities that are distinguished by the institution from other institutions through which the needs and expectations of the clients are met. (Idris; & Gallepi, 2009).

-Transformational Leadership: A process through which the leader and subordinates seek to advance each other to reach the highest levels of motivation and ethics. (Burns, 1978).

-Leadership Excellence: "The ability to motivate individuals to have the desire and are willingly committed to achieving or exceeding organizational goals" (Musa & Tulay, 2008, p.29).).

-Directorate of Education: It is the body responsible for the administration of education in the area located, headed by the Director of Education, and includes a number of administrative and technical departments.

Theoretical framework and previous studies:

Theoretical framework:

Introduction:
Perhaps the era of change markedly in different aspects of life, and the associated information and technological revolution that swept through all organizations of all kinds, and the provision of technology innovative ways to accomplish the educational tasks, which changed the form of the educational process and its goal and create a highly competitive environment called organizations To pay close attention to the nature of efforts to accomplish the work, to maximize effectiveness by focusing on the efforts of teachers beyond the limits of official roles and requirements (Che-Meh & Nasurdin, 2009). Transformational leadership is today one of the most well-known leadership theories of transformational organizations, the leadership needed by today's rapidly changing organizations. It is making radical changes by persuading subordinates to look beyond their own interests for the common good of the Organization, expand their interests and deepen the level of Their recognition and acceptance of the vision and goals of the organization through the influence of charisma, individual attention, and creative encouragement (Ameri, 2001).
The importance of organizational justice stems from its being an important and influential variable in the management processes in general, and educational management in particular, and their functions. It is seen as one of the organizational variables with a potential impact on the efficiency of the functioning of the employees of the organizations, as well as the performance of the organizations themselves. In this regard, Greenberg (1990) pointed out that organizational justice as a value, content, and variable has implications for organizational influence, and can explain many other variables influencing the organizational behavior of ILO staff, since organizational justice demonstrates how The members of the organization are judged on the fairness of the organization in dealing with them at the functional and humanitarian levels.
The distinguished institutions are keen to translate their vision, mission and strategic goals into reality in order to achieve their ambitions, through which they seek to support and encourage excellence and creativity from various activities and fields of work. It is important to emphasize at the outset that outstanding organizational performance is no longer an option for organizations. It is an imperative imposed on the organization by many external circumstances and forces, and excellence has no limits or inhibitions. Excellence is an administrative pattern of thought that can occur in a small or large organization, an organization that provides service or manufactures a commodity, governmental or non-governmental organization. In terms of changes, organizations are no longer required to perform only, but to excel in performance as a necessity for survival and sustainability. Performance represents the ability of organizations to achieve goals through optimal use of the resource and reflects the extent to which human resources perform their tasks according to specific criteria, So that the best performance is achieved. (Ghazi, 2014).

The concept of transformational management:
Transformational Leadership is a term that emerged in the field of leadership. The term was first introduced in 1978 by the American historian of politics and politics James Magregor Burns. Burns's theory of transformational management focused on the type of leadership required to move organizations And transform them to become more productive and computational (Hilali & Hilali, 2001). The theory of transformational management as mentioned in Al-Raqab (2010) is one of the prominent models in the new theories that have taken a major place. The process of developing subordinates and improving their performance was one of the main outputs of such leadership. The basic principle emphasizes the development of the subordinate and improving his performance. Within subordinates so as to increase their ability to fulfill current and future obligations required of them. The essence of transformational management focuses on the ability to harmonize means with goals and form and reshape institutions for great humanitarian purposes and ethical aspirations. This leadership model recognizes the apparent and underlying needs of subordinates and seeks to satisfy those needs and invest the maximum potential of subordinates in order to achieve intentional change (Ghamdi, 2000). And transformational management means the extent to which the administrative leader seeks to raise the level of his subordinates for self-development and development and to develop the groups and the organization as a whole (Hawari, 1996).

There is no definition agreed upon by educators and scholars because of different views and philosophies, but there is a clear agreement in the content concerned, and here we list the most important of these definitions:

(Bass & Avolio, 1993) defines it as:"Leadership that includes a number of interrelated components of charisma or ideal influence characteristics or behavior, inspirational motivation, intellectual or mental stimulation or stimulation, individual consideration, and transformational management behavior influences the change of subordinates' motivation , Turning subordinates so that they become more aware of the tasks required, and promote them to higher levels of needs, and transcend the circle of self-interest of individuals for the benefit of the organization (Otaibi, 2005, p. 4).

-Organizational Justice:
Adams (1965) defines organizational justice as equality, which involves an individual or employee comparing the rate of his output relative to his inputs with the rate of the output of other colleagues relative to their inputs, where the rates are equal, and where the rates are not equal, then the individual feels unfair. Within the management field, personnel management recognizes that there may be differences or gaps between employee perceptions and management perceptions of the existence of organizational justice in its various forms and presence. It therefore assumes that there is a conflict between workers' expectations and goals, and what management expects. In the light of this proposition, organizational justice becomes an acceptable mechanism to eliminate negative organizational conflict and to harmonize the common objectives of both staff and management. (Bardwell & Holden, 2001). Highlighting the types of organizational justice, (Niehoff & Moorman, 1993) noted that there are three types of organizational justice:

1.Distributive Justice: It is the justice of the outputs that the employee receives. Individuals evaluate the results of their actions according to a distributional rule based on the principle of equality.

2.Procedural Justice: It is the extent to which the worker feels the fairness of the procedures used in determining the outputs. The fairness of the proceedings is a mental perception of the fairness of the decision-making procedures that affect individuals. If the distribution justice relates to the fairness of the employee's outputs, the procedural fairness relates to the fairness of the procedures used in determining those outputs.

3.Interactional Justice: The extent to which a worker feels the fairness of the treatment he receives when he applies some formal procedures or knows the reasons for the application of these procedures, and notes that there is a close correlation between the fairness of the distribution, the fairness of the proceedings and the interactive justice. Affects the level of loyalty to the organization, the staff who feel the fairness of the procedures and the fairness of distribution and interactive justice have a high level of loyalty, so both the fairness of the procedures and the distribution and interactivity can affect the sense of workers of regulatory justice In many cases, the manner in which (Eg: evaluation of performance) can affect the person's sense of justice, hence the need for evaluation justice, which includes specific processes, procedures and systems that ensure that workers' rights and performance levels They are evaluated in a fair and fair manner, providing them with stability and job security.

-Institutional Excellence:
The definition of institutional excellence comes from many books, studies and research. This diversity reflects the importance of the concept that has made contemporary administrative approaches focused on defining the concepts of organizational excellence. The scientific administration has defined the concept of efficiency as the basis of organizational excellence and the entrance of human relations. Organizational processes, quality of life, climate and organizational culture. Administrative efforts have continued, including contemporary administrative approaches that have defined the concept of effectiveness that focuses on achieving the objectives of the Organization College under multilateral environmental changes. (Zayed, 2003).

The importance of institutional excellence lies in:
1.Organizations need ways and means to identify the obstacles they face.
2.Organizations need a means of gathering information, so that they can make important decisions about human resources such as who should be promoted? Who is an altruistic, proactive and performance-oriented employee?
3.The organization needs to develop its members on an ongoing basis, whether managers or staff, so that they can help make the organization more distinguished in performance, compared with the competing organizations.
4.Does the organization need to provide the necessary skills to decision-makers whether individual or group? And reflect on the sensitivity of the role played by and its importance in achieving creativity and excellence in organizations.

-Types of institutional excellence:
1.Leadership excellence: Higher leadership has a direct impact on excellence, through the development of individuals' abilities, and encouraging them to excellence and creativity, through excellence in leadership skills and effective working relationships, and the ability to think renewed and away from tradition, To new ideas. The distinguished leader is the one who can see many problems in the same situation. He is aware of mistakes, shortcomings and shortcomings. He feels the problems. The people who are increasingly sensitive to the shortcomings and problems in all situations are more likely to go through the research and writing. Probability will increase in front of them towards excellence. (Borghini, 2013).

2.Excellence in providing service: All categories of employees are consumers of goods and services, and when a commodity is not received does not meet the needs of the categories of customers or increase their expectations, these dealers resort to competitors to deal with them. In the management of excellence, resorting to these results is an indication that something is wrong in the method of service delivery that led to the production of this service, and these symptoms lead to a plan of action to correct these errors or shortcomings. (Nuaimi et al., 2008).

3.Human excellence: The organization is a meaningful human groupings, and management is the process of achieving organizational goals with a high degree of efficiency and effectiveness. (Daft, 2000). "Human resources" means all permanent and temporary employment in the Organization. In other words, the term employment refers to organizational leaders and heads of organizational units at all organizational levels. In this sense, the infrastructure of an organization is the human element. The importance of the human element is due to several reasons: human being is the decision-maker, responsible for innovation and innovation, and the mediator of learning in the Organization. Despite recent quantitative methods in organizational decision-making, the human element is the deciding factor in the decision-making process (Ghazi, 2014).

Previous studies:

-(Soud & Sultan, 2009) entitled "The degree of organizational justice among the heads of the academic departments in the official Jordanian universities and their relation to the organizational loyalty of faculty members"
The study aimed to identify the level of organizational justice among the heads of the academic departments in the official Jordanian universities and the relationship between organizational loyalty among faculty members. The study population is composed of all members of the full-time Jordanian teaching staff with a PhD degree in the Jordanian universities. The number of students is 2905 faculty members, while the sample of the study is randomly selected by 450 faculty members. In order to achieve the objectives of the study, two tools were used for teaching staff: the organizational justice scale, designed by Nihov and Norman, and in the final form of (26) paragraphs after adding a fourth dimension, and the measure of organizational loyalty prepared by Porter and his colleagues, (15) paragraph. The validity of the two measurements has been verified. The results of the study showed that the level of organizational justice among heads of academic departments is high. And that the level of organizational loyalty of teaching staff members is high. A positive and statistically significant relationship is found between the heads of the academic departments of organizational justice and the organizational loyalty of faculty members. The study came out with a number of recommendations.

-(Yilmaz, 2010) entitled "The perceptions of government secondary school teachers about organizational justice"
The study aimed to identify the perceptions of secondary school teachers about organizational justice according to the variables of gender, age, scientific qualification, years of experience, and scientific specialization. The sample of the study consisted of (322) teachers working in public schools in Turkey. The results of the study showed that the perceptions of the teachers about organizational justice in the school were high on the total number and ranged between the average and high on the different areas of organizational justice, There are differences in the level of teachers' perceptions of organizational justice according to sex variables and years of experience in favor of males and teachers with high experience, and there are no statistically significant

differences in this level according to the variables: scientific qualification, age and scientific specialization. The study came out with a number of recommendations.

-(Kim. 2010), "The Effect of Four Factors Contributing to Employees' Expectations on the Competitive Environment on Institutional Performance"
The study aimed at identifying the impact of four factors that contribute to the employees' expectations about the competitive environment on institutional performance. These factors are salaries, benefits, opportunities, and regulations. The sample of the study consisted of (60) workers working in NASP-III. The study reached many results, the most prominent of which is: a high contribution to the expectations of the employees about the competitive environment on the performance of their organization.

-(Edralin, 2010), entitled "Determining the degree to which human resources management practices are catalyzed for leadership in the largest companies in the Philippines".
The study aimed to determine the degree to which human resources management practices are motivated to achieve leadership, as well as to identify which HRM functions are most conducive to leadership in the largest companies in the Philippines. The study sample consisted of (300) employees working in (11) large companies in the Philippines. The study found that the sample companies applied many human resource practices related to human resources management functions. And that employee relations, training and development, polarization and selection contribute fairly to the leadership of these companies.

-(Hassan. 2010) entitled "Human Resource Management Practices and their Impact on Achieving Institutional Excellence- Applied Study in Zain Kuwait Mobile Telecommunications Company"
The study aimed to identify the impact of human resource management practices on achieving organizational excellence in Zain Kuwait Mobile Telecommunications Company. To achieve the objectives of the study, the researcher designed a questionnaire that included (40) paragraphs to collect the preliminary information from the sample of the study consisting of (253) individual. In light of this, data collection and analysis and hypothesis testing were carried out using the SPSS program. The study reached a number of results, most notably: (1). The presence of a significant impact of the polarization and recruitment in the achievement of leadership excellence and excellence in providing service at the level (0.05) in the Zain Kuwait Mobile Telecommunications Company. (2). The presence of a significant impact of training and development in achieving leadership excellence and excellence in providing service at the level (0.05) in the Zain Kuwait Mobile Telecommunications Company. (3). The presence of a significant impact of performance evaluation in achieving leadership excellence and excellence in providing service at (0.05) level in Zain Kuwait Mobile Telecommunications Company. (4). The presence of a significant impact of the compensations in achieving leadership excellence and excellence in providing service at (0.05) level in Zain Kuwait Mobile Telecommunications Company. (5). The presence of a significant impact on occupational health and safety in achieving leadership excellence and excellence in providing service at (0.05) level in Zain Kuwait Mobile Telecommunications Company. The study recommended that: (1). Reinforcing the interest of Zain Kuwait for cellular communications is very important for ISO staff training. The senior management of Kuwait Telecommunications Company (Zain) has always sought to achieve a competitive position.

-(Ahamdi, 2011) entitled "The relationship between organizational justice and the behavior of organizational citizenship in food industry organizations in the Kurdistan Region"

The study aimed to identify the analysis of the correlation between the perception of organizational justice and the behavior of organizational citizenship in a number of food factories in the Kurdistan region of Iraq. The results of 73 of the owners of these factories indicated that the distribution, While the results did not show a positive relationship between the fairness of information and the behavior of organizational citizenship. The study came out with a number of recommendations.

-(Abu Haddaf, 2011) entitled "The Role of Transformational Management in Developing the Effectiveness of Teaching Teachers in UNRWA Schools in Gaza Governorates".

The study aimed to know the role of transformational management in developing the effectiveness of teaching teachers in UNRWA schools in Gaza governorates. The sample consisted of (412) teachers and teachers of the preparatory stage in the schools of UNRWA, through the use of a questionnaire consisting of (66) paragraph distributed to (6) areas, according to descriptive analytical approach. The study found that there are statistically significant differences between the average scores of the sample members on the role of transformational management in the development of the effectiveness of teachers attributed to the gender variable and the differences were in favor of females. The absence of statistically significant differences between the average scores of the sample members on the role of transformational management in developing the effectiveness of teachers attributed to the variable of scientific qualification. The study showed statistically significant differences between the average scores of the sample members on the role of transformational management in the development of the effectiveness of teachers due to variable years of experience and the differences in favor of less than (5) years. Finally, the study showed that there were statistically significant differences between the average scores of the sample members on the role of the transformational administration in developing the effectiveness of the teachers due to the conservative variable. The differences were in favor of Rafah governorate at the expense of Khan Yunis. The study came out with a number of recommendations.

-(Barakat, 2014) entitled "The Degree of Organizational Justice for Public School Principals in Palestine from the Perspective of their School Teachers"

The study aimed at determining the degree of organizational justice among the principals of public schools in Palestine from the point of view of their school teachers and indicating the difference between the responses of these teachers in the level of organizational justice among their school principals according to the variables of gender, specialization, qualification and experience. The sample of the study consisted of (284) teachers and teachers. The results of the study showed that the perceptions of the teachers about the organizational justice of their school principals were high, in the sub-fields and the total number. The results of the study showed that there were differences in the level of teachers' perceptions about organizational justice according to the variable years of experience on the field of distributive justice and the total sum in favor of the category of teachers with high experience. The results showed no significant differences in these perceptions on procedural and interactive justice, There are no significant differences in the perceptions of teachers about organizational justice in the sub-fields and the total number according to the variables of gender, specialization and scientific qualification. The study came out with a number of recommendations.

-(Buhaisi. 2014) entitled "The Role of Empowering Employees in Achieving Institutional Excellence/A Field Study on Technical Colleges in the Governorates of the Gaza Strip"

The study aimed to identify the role of empowering employees in achieving organizational excellence in the technical colleges in the Gaza Strip. To achieve the objectives of the study, a questionnaire is developed consisting of (62) paragraphs for the purpose of collecting data. The sample consisted of (205) technical staff members in the Gaza Strip. The sample included administrative staff and academics in these colleges. The questionnaire included two main axes: one measures the degree of empowerment (organizational culture, delegation, information sharing, and work teams) Organizational Excellence (Leadership Excellence, Human Excellence, and Service Excellence), the researcher used a random stratified sample, and the results of the study were as follows: (1) The respondents in the sample agree on the availability of administrative empowerment in their colleges, First, followed by delegation of authority, participation in information, and after organizational culture in the last rank. (2) The respondents in the technical colleges agree on the availability of institutional excellence in all dimensions (leadership, human and service). (Leadership excellence, human excellence, and service excellence). (3) The results showed that there is a statistically significant relationship between organizational culture, administrative authority, participation of information and work teams on the one hand, and leadership, human and service excellence on the other. The results showed that there is a statistically significant relationship in the role of empowerment in achieving organizational excellence due to the following variables: (college, general level, years of service and age) .5 The results also indicated a statistically significant relationship between empowerment in achieving excellence The gender variable and for males The study includes a number of recommendations, the most important of which are: (The need for organizational culture, administrative authority, participation of information and work teams to achieve institutional excellence, and to provide and intensify continuous training courses for the employees of information technology and analysis, increase confidence and support among employees during the mandate period, And to increase the courses that are concerned with introducing employees to the concept of excellence and adopting it as a strategy, and to adopt strategic goals in the leadership of the faculties that are working to meet the demands of the student public to serve in these colleges, Financial allocations that support programs of excellence in the faculties, and work on the emancipation of outstanding employees in colleges in all fields.

Comment on previous studies:

After the previous review of previous Arab and foreign studies, the researcher concluded that the issue of the topic of transformational management and its application in institutions has received the attention of researchers, where many studies dealt with the role of transformational management in achieving employee satisfaction and development of their effectiveness, such as (Abu Haddaf, 2011) study, also the researcher concluded that the issue of organizational justice and their role in achieving job satisfaction and organizational loyalty, which leads to improvement in the performance of the institution has received the attention of a number of researchers such as the study of (Soud and Sultan, 2009), (Yilmaz, 2010). Other studies have dealt with the relationship between organizational justice and citizenship behavior, such as (Ahamdi, 2011). Other studies have also dealt with the role of organizational justice, Several variables in achieving institutional excellence such as (Hassan, 2010), (Bohaisi, 2014), (Kim, 2010), (Edralin, 2010). The researcher benefited from these studies in identifying the fields of study and their variables and the statistical methods in analyzing their results, as well as in constructing the items of the questionnaire and its fields and paragraphs. And benefited from the findings, recommendations and proposals of these studies. These studies have enriched this study with the expertise contained there. The most important characteristic of this study is that it is concerned with Practice of transformational management, and the degree of organizational justice and their roles in achieving institutional excellence from the point of view of workers in the directorates of education in Hebron from the point of view of those who influence and are influenced by the educational process. In addition to its uniqueness in the study of Practice of transformational management and the degree of organizational justice and their roles in achieving institutional excellence from the point of view of the staff of the directorates of education in Hebron, this gives a clear picture of the organization's organizational status and the importance of Practice of transformational management and achieving organizational justice in the directorates of education Which lead the formation of students and builders of the future, which is an incentive for leaders of those institutions to achieve institutional excellence.

Study Methodology:
This study is conducted during the month of June 2017. The researcher used the analytical descriptive approach as the method that describes the phenomenon and studies it and collects the accurate data and information and its suitability for this type of studies.

Study population:
The study population consists of all employees in the directorates of education in Hebron with (369) employees working in four districts (north Hebron, Hebron, south of Hebron, Yatta).

Study sample:
The researcher distributed the study tool to a sample of workers in the directorates of education in Hebron(North Hebron, Hebron, South Hebron, Yatta). The number of questionnaires retrieved from the field (103) is (22.8%). The total population is a statistically representative sample. Table (1) shows the distribution of the study sample.

Table (1): Distribution of Study Sample Individuals by Study Variables.

No	Variables		Number	Percentage %
1	Gender	Male	72	69.9
		Female	31	30.1
2	Age	Less than 30 years	8	7.8
		From 30 to less than 40 years	40	38.8
		From 40 to less than 50 years	37	35.9
		50 years and over	18	17.5
3	Qualification	Diploma and less	9	8.7
		BA	73	70.9
		Master and above	21	20.4
4	Job title	administrative employee	43	41.8
		Educational Supervisor	31	30
		Head of the Department	29	28.2
5	Years of service	Less than 5 years	10	9.7
		from 5 - less than 10 years	25	24.3
		from 10 - Less than 15 years	19	18.5
		15 years and above	49	47.5
6	Directorate	North Hebron	24	23.3
		Hebron	23	22.3
		South Hebron	30	29.1
		Yatta	26	25.3

Study Tool:

The researcher prepared a questionnaire to measure the Achieving institutional excellence through organizational justice and transformational management from the point of view of workers in the directorates of education in Hebron, based on the literature and previous studies. The questionnaire consisted of four sections:

Section1:

This section contains the initial data of the employee who fills the questionnaire, namely: (gender, age, scientific qualification, job title, years of service, Directorate).

Section2:

The degree of organizational justice in the directorates of education in Hebron from the point of view of its employees, and consists of four main areas and (33) paragraph on the hypotheses of research and answer the questions of the study has been the answer of these paragraphs (I strongly agree, I agree, unsure , I disagree, strongly disagree).

Section 3:

The degree of the practice of transformational management from the point of view of workers in the directorates of education in Hebron governorate, and it consists of four fields and (41) paragraphs on the hypotheses of research and answer the questions of the study has been the answer of these paragraphs (I strongly agree, I agree, unsure , I disagree, strongly disagree).

Section 4: It measures the degree of institutional excellence in the directorates of education in Hebron from the point of view of its employees. It consists of three main areas and (24) paragraphs dealing with the hypotheses of research and answering the study questions. The responses of these sections (I strongly agree, , I disagree, strongly disagree), and this questionnaire is divided as shown in Table (2).

Table (2): Fields of Study.

No	Areas	Number of paragraphs
	The degree of the practice of transformational management from the point of view of workers in the directorates of education in Hebron .	
1	The ideal effect	11
2	Inspirational stimulation	10
3	Thought provoking	10
4	Attention to the individual	10
	Total	41
	The degree of organizational justice in the directorates of education in Hebron from the point of view of its employees, and consists of four fields:	
1	Procedural justice	8
2	Distributive justice	10
3	Interactive Justice	9
4	Evaluation justice	6
	Total	33
	The level of institutional excellence in the directorates of education in Hebron from the perspective of its employees, and consists of three fields:	
1	Leadership excellence	9
2	Human excellence	9
3	Excellence in service delivery	6
	Total	24

Validation of the Tool:

The validity of the tool expresses the validity of the tool used to measure what is set for measurement. The researcher presented the questionnaire to a number of specialists and experienced in a number of Palestinian universities with PhDs and Masters. The paragraphs of the questionnaire were amended according to the proposed observations and amendments, The questionnaire is finalized accordingly, so that the number of paragraphs of the questionnaire becomes final (98).

Stability of the Tool:

To verify the stability of the measuring instrument, the internal consistency and stability of the resolution paragraphs were examined by calculating the Cronbach 'alpha' factor, according to Tables (3,4,5).

Table (3): Stability coefficients for the study dimensions of Practice of transformational management according to stability coefficients.

Fields of study	Number of paragraphs	Value of alpha
The ideal effect	11	0.877
Inspirational stimulation	10	0.912
Thought provoking	10	0.911
Attention to the individual	10	0.921
Total score	41	0.967

Table (3) shows, the coefficients of the stability of the study instrument in all study fields ranged between (0.877) and (0.921). The field of Attention to the individual obtained the highest stability coefficient, while The ideal effect obtained the lowest stability coefficient, Alpha value on the total score (0.967), indicating the accuracy of the measuring instrument.

Table (4): Stability coefficients for the study dimensions of organizational justice according to stability coefficients.

Fields of study	Number of paragraphs	Value of alpha
Procedural justice	8	0.821
Distributive justice	10	0.912
Interactive Justice	9	0.895
Evaluation justice	6	0.835
Total score	33	0.958

Table (4) shows, the coefficients of the stability of the study instrument in all study fields ranged between (0.821) and (0.912). The field of distributive justice obtained the highest stability coefficient, while procedural justice obtained the lowest stability coefficient, Alpha value on the total score (0.958), indicating the accuracy of the measuring instrument.

Table (5): Stability coefficients for the dimensions of the study of institutional excellence according to stability coefficients.

Fields of study	Number of paragraphs	Value of alpha
Leadership excellence	9	0.927
Human excellence	9	0.928
Excellence in service delivery	6	0.905
Total score	24	0.967

Table (5) shows that the coefficients of the stability of the study instrument in all fields of study ranged between (0.905) and (0.928). The field of human excellence obtained the highest stability coefficient, while the field of excellence in service delivery has the lowest stability coefficient. Finally, the total value of alpha is (0.967), indicating the accuracy of the measuring instrument.

Study Procedures:

After verifying the validity and stability of the study tool, and determining the sample, it is agreed to conduct such a study, and to allow the distribution of the questionnaire to the workers in the directorates of education in Hebron governorate, where (200) questionnaires were distributed and (103) were recovered.

Statistical processing:

After collecting the study data, the researcher reviewed it as a prelude to the introduction of the computer and is introduced to the computer by giving them specific numbers, that is to convert the verbal responses to digital where the answer is given strongly agree five degrees, the answer I agree four grades, the answer is not sure three degrees, I disagree with two degrees, and the answer is not strongly agree to one degree. In all the paragraphs of the study and thus became the questionnaire measures administrative transparency in the Ministry of Education from the point of view of workers in the directorates of education in Hebron in positive direction. Statistical analysis of the data is done by extracting numbers, arithmetical averages, standard deviations, T-test, one way Anova, cronbach alpha, linear regression analysis using SPSS.

Study results, discussion, interpretation and recommendations

This study deals with the findings of the researcher through the response of the members of the study sample on organizational justice and its role in achieving institutional excellence in the directorates of education in Hebron from the point of view of its employees according to the study questions and hypotheses. The reference to phrases in the study tool (questionnaire) is as follows:

Table (6): Mean of the arithmetic mean.

Mean	Arithmetic mean
1.00-1.80	Very low
1.81-2.61	Low
2.62-3.42	Medium
3.43-4.23	High
4.24-5.00	Very high

In light of the processing of the study data statistically, the researcher reached the following results:

Q 1) What is the degree of organizational justice in the directorates of education in Hebron from the point of view of its employees?

Table (7): Arithmetical Means and Standard Deviations of the Degree of Organizational Justice in the Directorates of Education in Hebron from the Point of View of its Employees by Field of Study.

Fields of study	Mean	Std deviation	Grade
Procedural justice	3.02	0.708	Medium
Distributive justice	3.15	0.758	Medium
Interactive Justice	3.35	0.762	Medium
Evaluation justice	3.12	0.758	Medium
Organizational justice in general	3.17	0.673	Medium

Table (7) shows that the level of organizational justice in the directorates of education in Hebron from the point of view of its employees is generally medium with an average (3.17) and a std deviation (0.673). The highest fields is organizational justice with average (3.75), std deviation (0.762), followed by distributive justice with average (3.15) , std deviation (0.758) followed by evaluation justice with average (3.13),std deviation (0.758), Finally Procedural justice with average (3.02), std Deviation (0.708). The researcher attributed the reason to the lack of environmental conditions (internal and external) appropriate and appropriate for workers in the directorates of education, and this is due to several reasons, including: lack of salaries, the lack of an effective system of incentives, weak professionalism in dealing and others).

Q2: What is the degree of procedural justice in the directorates of education in Hebron from the perspective of its employees?

Table (8): Mathematical Meanings and Standard Deviations of the Degree of Procedural Justice in the Directorates of Education in Hebron, by Study Paragraphs.

Study paragraph	mean	Std deviation	Grade	Field
I feel that my duties and duties are appropriate	3.51	1.01	High	
I feel comfortable with what I earn and what I have	2.68	1.15	Medium	
I think the financial incentives provided are appropriate	2.26	1.10	Low	
I feel that the responsibilities given me are appropriate	3.32	1.01	Medium	
There is a similarity between the salaries and salaries of those who look at me	2.67	1.19	Medium	Procedural Justice
The Directorate has clear laws and regulations that facilitate compliance	3.39	0.932	Medium	
The Directorate shall provide all necessary to facilitate the work procedures	3.19	0.990	Medium	
Employees receive all their entitlements during and after service	3.12	1.07	Medium	
The degree of procedural fairness in general	3.02	0.708	Medium	

Table(8) shows that the level of procedural justice in the directorates of education in Hebron from the point of view of its employees is medium with average (3.02), std deviation (0.708). The paragraph "I feel that my duties and duties are appropriate" is high with average (3.51), std deviation (1.01) while the paragraph "I think the financial incentives offered to me is appropriate" is low, with average (2.26), std deviation (1.10).

Q3) What is the degree of distributive justice in the directorates of education in Hebron from the point of view of its employees?

Table (9): The Statistical Meanings and Standard Deviations of the Distributive Justice Degree in the Directorates of Education in Hebron by Paragraphs of the Study.

Study paragraph	mean	Std deviation	Grade	Field
Decision makers take action in a fair manner	3.17	1.05	Medium	
It is my responsibility to ensure that each member shows his opinion before taking action decisions	3.14	0.953	Medium	
The administrator collects accurate and complete information before making business decisions	3.05	0.978	Medium	
The official explains all the details to the members if they are asked about this	3.25	1.01	Medium	
Administrative decisions are applied to all members without exception	2.88	1.11	Medium	
The administrator allows objections to the decisions he makes	3.27	1.03	Medium	
The official responsible gives the employees the right to leave	3.81	0.871	High	Distributive justice
The official grants part of his powers to the workers according to his specialties	3.60	0.878	High	
The officer applies the methods of dress and punishment in a fair and balanced manner	2.95	1.06	Medium	
I feel that the civil service law gives me appropriate incentives	2.42	1.15	Low	
The degree of distributive justice in general	3.15	0.758	Medium	

Table (9) shows that the level of distributive justice in the directorates of education in Hebron is medium with average (3.15), std deviation (0.758). The paragraph "The official responsible gives the employees the right to leave "with average (3.81), std deviation (0.871), and the paragraph" the official grants part of his powers to the workers according to his specialties "with average of (3.60),std deviation (0.878) is high, while The paragraph "I feel that the civil service law gives me appropriate incentives" with average (2.42) , std deviation (1.15) is low.

Q4) What is the degree of interactive justice in the directorates of education in Hebron from the point of view of its employees?

Table (10): Mathematical Meanings and Standard Deviations of the Degree of Interactive Justice in the Directorates of Education in Hebron by Paragraphs of Study.

Study paragraph	mean	Std deviation	Grade	Field
I have the opportunity to participate in decision-making related to my work	3.35	1.09	Medium	
I am treated with all due respect by Wood and with regard to the decisions concerning my work	3.41	0.955	Medium	
The official shows interest in my concurrence with regard to the decisions related to my work	3.39	0.993	Medium	
The official discusses with me the consequences of decisions that can affect my work.	3.41	1.01	Medium	
The official is responsible for the participation of staff in professional meetings	3.38	1.00	Medium	Interactive Justice
The official shows interest in workers' professional rights	3.21	1.01	Medium	
Delegation of some administrative responsibilities to some members	3.51	1.00	High	
I feel that the official deals with all those who work with democracy	3.19	1.12	Medium	
I feel that my career is related to the nature of my relationship with the official	3.29	1.07	Medium	
The degree of interactive justice in general	3.35	0.762	Medium	

Table (10) shows that the level of interactive justice in the directorates of education in Hebron from the point of view of its employees is medium with average (3.35), std deviation (0.762). The paragraph " Delegation of some administrative responsibilities to some members "with average (3.51) ,std deviation (1.00), while all other paragraphs were medium.

Q5) What is the degree of evaluation justice in the directorates of education in Hebron from the point of view of its employees?

Table (11): The Statistical Meanings and the Standard Deviations of the Degree of Evaluating Justice in the Directorates of Education in Hebron by Study Paragraphs.

Study paragraph	mean	std deviation	Grade	Field
I have the right opportunity to upgrade whenever I am distinguished in my work	2.72	1.08	Medium	
Performance is assessed by a responsible, transparent and objective person away from personal biases.	3.11	1.11	Medium	
I have knowledge of the criteria by which my performance is assessed.	3.54	0.987	High	
I have the opportunity to object to a performance evaluation if i feels unfair	3.60	0.921	High	Evaluation justice
Performance appraisal is based on what employees have achieved	3.14	1.04	Medium	
The official is keen to reward outstanding employees for performance	2.60	0.983	Low	
The degree of Evaluation justice in general	3.12	0.758	Medium	

Table (11) shows that the level of evaluation justice in the directorates of education in Hebron from the point of view of its employees is medium with average (3.12), std deviation (0.758). The paragraph "I have the opportunity to object to a performance evaluation if I feel unfair "with average(3.60),std deviation (0.921) and a paragraph " I have knowledge of the criteria by which my performance is assessed" with average (3.54), std deviation (0.978) is high, while the paragraph "the official is keen to reward outstanding employees for Performance " is low with average (2.60), std deviation (0.983).

Q6) What is the degree of institutional excellence in the directorates of education in Hebron from the point of view of its employees?.

Table (12): The Mean and Standard Deviations of the Degree of Institutional Excellence in the Directorates of Education in Hebron from the Point of View of Employees by Field of Study.

Fields of study	Mean	Std deviation	Grade
Leadership excellence	3.25	0.780	Medium
Human excellence	2.86	0.896	Medium
Excellence in service delivery	3.18	0.886	Medium
Institutional excellence in general	3.07	0.798	Medium

Table (12) shows that the level of institutional excellence in the directorates of education in Hebron from the point of view of its employees is generally medium with average (3.07) , std deviation (0.798). The highest field of institutional excellence is Leadership excellence with average (3.25), std deviation (0.780), followed by the field of excellence in service delivery with average (3.18), std deviation (0.886), and finally the field of human excellence with average (2.86), std deviation (0.896). The researcher attributed the reason to the lack of interest by the employees in achieving the institutional excellence of the departments they work in. This is due to the lack of real competition between these departments as public institutions, and also due to the lack of regulatory justice in the required form within these districts.

Q7) What is the degree of leadership excellence in the directorates of education in Hebron from the point of view of its employees?

Table (13): The arithmetic averages and standard deviations of the degree of leadership excellence in the directorates of education in Hebron, according to the study paragraphs.

Study paragraph	mean	Std deviation	Grade	Field
The management of the Directorate confirms compliance with the provisions of institutional excellence	3.22	0.989	Medium	
The Directorate will manage the planning of future needs	3.37	0.940	Medium	
The management of the Directorate adopts strategic objectives according to the needs of its clients	3.32	0.898	Medium	
The administration of the Directorate adopts the strategic objectives according to the needs of the employees of the Directorate	3.25	0.967	Medium	
the Directorate is concerned with the establishment of specialized courses aimed at introducing employees at all administrative levels to the importance of serving the public and excellence in service delivery	3.13	1.00	Medium	Leadership excellence
The management of the Directorate continuously seeks excellence in providing service to the public	3.53	0.883	High	
The management of the Directorate encourages staff to provide distinct ideas	3.33	1.01	Medium	
The management of the Directorate works to motivate employees to provide excellent services	3.00	1.06	Medium	
The Directorate of the Directorate seeks to adopt the philosophy of change as needed	3.10	1.02	Medium	
The grade of leadership excellence in general	3.25	0,780	Medium	

Table (13) shows that the level of leadership excellence in the directorates of education in Hebron from the point of view of its employees is medium with average (3.25), std deviation (0.780). The paragraph "The management of the directorate continuously seeks excellence in providing service to the public" is high with average (3.53) and a standard deviation of (0.883). Otherwise all paragraphs is medium.

Q8) What is the degree of human excellence in the directorates of education in Hebron from the point of view of its employees?

Table (14): Mathematical Meanings and Standard Deviations of the Degree of Human Excellence in the Directorates of Education in Hebron by Study Paragraphs.

Study paragraph	mean	Std deviation	Grade	Field
The Directorate develops the competencies of its employees to achieve excellence and creativity	3.06	1.08	Medium	
The Directorate attracts qualified people to work there	2.92	1.12	Medium	
The Directorate provides its staff with modern tools to help them carry out their work with high quality	3.23	1.12	Medium	
Employees receive rewards commensurate with their assessment	2.36	1.13	Low	
The Directorate offers the opportunity to send distinguished employees	2.52	1.17	Low	
The Directorate uses effective programs to integrate new employees into the workforce	2.95	1.17	Medium	Human excellence
The Directorate shall periodically assess the job satisfaction of its employees	2.79	1.11	Medium	
The Directorate shall ensure the good investment of the employees	3.00	0.954	Medium	
The Directorate allocates a special budget for the implementation of social activities.	2.86	1.21	Medium	
The degree of human excellence in general	2.86	0.896	Medium	

Table (14) shows that the level of human excellence in the directorates of education in Hebron from the point of view of its employees is medium with average (2.86), std deviation (0.896). The paragraph "Employees receive rewards commensurate with their assessment " with average (2.36), std deviation (1.13) , and the paragraph "The Directorate offers the opportunity to send distinguished employees" with average (2.52), std deviation (1.17) is low, while the rest of the paragraphs to a medium degree.

Q9) What is the degree of excellence in providing service in the directorates of education in Hebron from the point of view of its employees?

Table (15): Mathematical Meanings and Standard Deviations of Degree of Excellence in Service Delivery in the Directorates of Education in Hebron Governorate, by Study Paragraphs.

Study paragraph	mean	Std deviation	Grade	Field
The Directorate conducts ongoing surveys to identify the needs of its clients	2.87	1.12	Medium	
Service delivery is subject to continuous tuning and improvement	2.99	1.07	Medium	
The Directorate adopts modern technological means in providing its services	3.40	1.07	Medium	
Service delivery procedures are fast and comfortable	3.23	1.07	Medium	Excellence in service delivery
The Directorate continuously monitors its facilities to improve service delivery mechanisms	3.22	1.02	Medium	
The Directorate encourages staff feedback to upgrade services	3.00	1.08	Medium	
The degree of excellence in providing the service in general	3.18	0.886	Medium	

Table (15) shows that the level of excellence in providing service in the directorates of education in Hebron from the point of view of its employees is medium with average (3.18), std deviation (0.886). while the rest of all paragraphs to a medium degree.

Testing the main question2:
what is the practice of transformational management and its role in achieving organizational excellence from the perspective of working in school districts in Hebron?, and the following sub-questions arise from it:
Q1) What is the degree of the practice of transformational management from the point of view of workers in the directorates of education in Hebron governorate?

Table (16): Arithmetical Means and Standard Deviations of the Degree of transformational management in the Directorates of Education in Hebron from the Point of View of Employees by Field of Study.

Fields of study	Mean	Std deviation	Grade
The ideal effect	3.05	0.707	Medium
Inspirational stimulation	3.15	0.758	Medium
Thought provoking	3.37	0.767	Medium
Attention to the individual	3.03	0.794	Medium
Transformational management in general	3.15	0.679	Medium

Table (16) shows by the response of the sample members of the study, the degree of the practice of transformational management from the point of view of workers in the directorates of education was average, on the total score with an average of (3.15) and a standard deviation of (0.679). (3.75) and standard deviation (0.767), followed by the field of inspirational stimulation with mean (3.15) and standard deviation (0.758), followed by the ideal effect with mean (3.05) and standard deviation (0.707) my account (3.03) and standard deviation (0.794), and the researcher attributed the reason for those results to The emergence of transformational leadership patterns in public institutions, and the reluctance to delegate authority by managers because of excessive centralization in the work.

Table (17): Arithmetical Means and Standard Deviations of the Degree of transformational management in the Directorates of Education in Hebron from the Point of View of Employees by paragraph of Study.

Study paragraph	mean	Std deviation	Grade
He is interested in giving incentives to make change.	3.81	0.871	High
It gives us meaning to work by motivating and encouraging us.	3.60	0.878	High
Taking into account the individual differences between us in the area of needs and desires.	3.60	0.921	High
Maintains communication and communication with us according to our opinions and affiliations.	3.54	0.987	High
Addresses the difficulties facing the development of courageous action.	3.51	1.01	High
It gives us time to listen to our thoughts.	3.51	1.00	High
It stimulates thinking to solve problems.	3.51	1.00	High
Depends on constructive criticism when you fail to solve problems.	3.41	0.955	Medium
Allows for a significant amount of calculated risk in decision making.	3.41	1.01	Medium
He makes the team feel he belongs to him and his ideas.	3.39	0.932	Medium
We feel the truth of his words through his actions.	3.39	0.932	Medium
It allows the circulation of conflicting ideas to reach the optimal way.	3.39	0.993	Medium

Encourages the use of new methods of action.	3.38	1.00	Medium
Everyone is involved in the process of change.	3.35	1.09	Medium
He renews his ideas and aspires to change.	3.32	1.01	Medium
His words are consistent with his actions.	3.32	1.01	Medium
Authorizes the powers of the employees.	3.29	1.07	Medium
Justify the desired changes in a logical manner.	3.27	1.03	Medium
He accomplishes his duties with the participation of his staff.	3.25	1.01	Medium
It depends on constructive criticism and reinforcement with everything I do	3.21	1.01	Medium
Share with us the dangers.	3.19	0.990	Medium
His style of work is based on inspiring creativity and creativity in us.	3.19	1.12	Medium
It instills in us a sense of the objectives of the institution and the ministry and its objectives.	3.17	1.05	Medium
He builds the team to have human skills.	3.14	0.953	Medium
Taking into account the feelings of workers with their differences.	3.14	1.04	Medium
Depends on the modern administrative methods in the department management.	3.14	1.04	Medium
It offers our needs to its needs in several situations.	3.12	1.07	Medium
He listens attentively to every talk he has.	3.11	1.11	Medium
Weave intimate relationships with us, thus strengthening the social fabric.	3.11	1.11	Medium
His behavior with us raises our morale and progresses our work.	3.05	0.978	Medium
It drives us towards using IT as the fastest learning method.	2.95	1.06	Medium
It drives us to change.	2.88	1.11	Medium
Attention to our personal needs at the top of his priorities.	2.72	1.08	Medium
The performance of his staff as he possesses the technical skills for that.	2.72	1.08	Medium
Make important decisions with caution.	2.68	1.15	Medium
Distancing itself from personal gain.	2.68	1.15	Medium
We like him in every work he does.	2.67	1.19	Medium
Initiate the process of delegating work, to check on the progress of work and success.	2.60	0.983	Low
Everyone trusts a lot.	2.60	0.983	Low
It raises the challenge and stability.	2.42	1.15	Low
His good treatment of us obliges us to respect him.	2.26	1.10	Low
The grade of transformational management in general	3.15	0.679	Medium

Table (17), shows the highest paragraphs in the field of transformational management practice were:

-Interested in giving incentives to make the change, with an average of (3.81) and a standard deviation of (0.871).

-gives us meaning to work by stimulating and encouraging us, with an average of 3.60 and a standard deviation of 0.878.

-Consider the individual differences between us in the area of needs and desires, with an average of (3.60) and a standard deviation (0.921).

-Maintains communication and communication with us according to our opinions and affiliations, with an average of (3.54) and a standard deviation (0.987).

-addresses the difficulties facing the development of work courageously, with an average of (3.51) and a standard deviation (1.01).

-gives us time to listen to our ideas, with an average of (3.51) and a standard deviation (1.00).
-It works to stimulate thinking to solve problems, with an average of (3.51) and a standard deviation (1.00).

While the lowest paragraphs in the practice of transformational management were:
-His good treatment with us obligates us to respect him, with an average of (2.26) and a standard deviation of (1.10).
-raises the challenge and stability, with an average of (2.42) and a standard deviation (1.15).
-Everyone is very confident, with an average of (2.60) and a standard deviation of (0.983).
-Initiate the process of delegation of work, to check on the progress of work and success, with an average of (2.60) and a standard deviation (0.983).

Test hypothesis of the study:
*" *There are no statistically significant differences at the level of significance (α ≤0.05) in the degree of organizational justice and its role in achieving institutional excellence in the directorates of education in Hebron from the point of view of its employees according to the variables: (gender, Age, scientific qualification, job title, years of service, Directorate)", To answer this hypothesis, the arithmetical averages and standard deviations, the results of the T- test, and the results of the single-variance analysis test were extracted. This is shown in Tables 18-24.

Table (18): Results of the "T" test to indicate the differences in the degree of organizational justice and its role in achieving institutional excellence in the directorates of education in Hebron from the point of view of its employees according to the variable: gender.

Variables	Gender	Number	Mean	Std Deviation	df	T value	Sig (2-tailed
Organizational justice And achieving institutional excellence	Male	72	3.25	0.662	71	2.01	0.047
	Female	31	2.97	0.666	30		

Function at the level of significance(α≤0.05)

Table (18) showed that there were statistically significant differences in the degree of organizational justice and its role in achieving institutional excellence from the point of view of workers in the directorates of education in Hebron due to the gender variable. The statistical significance is < 0.05, which is a statistical function, The differences were in favor of males. The researcher attributed this to the increase in the number of males in the study sample, or perhaps because of the increase in male needs for females, and thus they are more concerned with achieving organizational justice than females.

Table (19): The mean and standard deviations, the results of the test and the results of the test of the analysis of the single variance to indicate the differences in the degree of organizational justice and its role in achieving the institutional excellence in the directorates of education in Hebron from the point of view of its employees according to the variable: Age.

Fields	Age	NO	Mean	Std. Deviation	Source of variance	Sum of squares	df	Mean square	F	Sig
Organizational justice and achieving institutional excellence	Less than 30 years	8	3.43	1.02	Between groups	0.856	3	0.285	0.622	0.602
	From 30 to less than 40 years	40	3.09	0.656						
	From 40- to less than 50 years	37	3.21	0.656	Within groups	45.391	99	0.458		
	50 years and over	18	3.14	0.582						
	Total	103	3.17	0.673	Total	46.247	102			

Table (19) shows that the results of the study showed that there were no statistically significant differences in the degree of organizational justice and its role in achieving institutional excellence from the point of view of workers in the directorates of education in Hebron due to the variable age, Where the statistical significance > 0.05 is not statistically significant. The researcher attributed this to the fact that the sense of organizational justice and the functional stability provided by the employees is not related to the age of the employee but to the degree of employee satisfaction and belonging to the institution.

Table (20): The arithmetical averages, standard deviations, test results and the results of the analysis of the single variance analysis to indicate differences in the degree of organizational justice and its role in achieving the institutional excellence in the directorates of education in Hebron from the point of view of their employees according to the variable: qualification .

Fields	qualification	NO	Mean	Std. Deviation	Source of variance	Sum of squares	df	Mean square	F	Sig
Organizational justice and achieving institutional excellence	Diploma and less	9	3.30	0.848	Between groups	0.545	2	0.260	0.569	0.568
	BA	73	3.19	0.628	Within groups	45.727	100	0.457		
	Master and above	21	3.04	0.758						
	Total	103	3.17	0.673	Total	46.247	102			

Table (20) shows that the results of the study showed that there were no statistically significant differences in the degree of organizational justice and its role in achieving institutional excellence from the point of view of workers in the directorates of education in Hebron due to the qualification. where the statistical significance> 0.05 is not statistically significant. The researcher attributed this to the fact that the sense of organizational justice and the functional stability provided by the employees is not related to the employee's scientific qualifications, but to the degree of employee satisfaction and belonging to his institution.

Table (21): Mathematical averages, standard deviations, test results and the results of the analysis of the single variance analysis to indicate the differences in the degree of organizational justice and its role in achieving the institutional excellence in the directorates of education in Hebron from the point of view of its employees according to the variable: Job title.

Fields	Job title	NO	Mean	Std. Deviation	Source of variance	Sum of squares	df	Mean square	F	Sig
Organizational justice and achieving institutional excellence	administrative employee	43	3.24	0.747	Between groups	0.572	2	0.286	0.626	0.537
	Educational Supervisor	31	3.06	0.545						
	Head of the Department	29	3.18	0.689	Within groups	45.675	100	0.457		
	Total	103	3.17	0.673	Total	46.247	102			

Table (21) shows that the results of the study showed that there were no statistically significant differences in the degree of organizational justice and its role in achieving institutional excellence from the point of view of workers in the directorates of education in Hebron due to the variable job title. where the statistical significance> 0.05 is not statistically significant. The researcher attributed this to the fact that the sense of organizational justice and the availability of functional stability in the employees is not related to the location of the employee in the hierarchy, but to the degree of employee satisfaction and belonging to the institution.

Table (22): The arithmetical averages, the standard deviations, the results of the test and the results of the analysis of the single variance analysis to indicate the differences in the degree of organizational justice and its role in achieving the institutional excellence in the directorates of education in Hebron from the point of view of the employees according to the variable: years of service.

Fields	Years of service	NO	Mean	Std. Deviation	Source of variance	Sum of squares	df	Mean square	F	Sig
Organizational justice and achieving institutional excellence	Less than 5 years	10	3.63	0.412	Between groups	4.142	3	1.367	3.312	0.026
	From 5 - less than 10 years	25	2.89	0.704						
	from 10 - less than 15 years	19	3.21	0.654						
	15 years and above	49	3.19	0.661	Within groups	42.145	99	0.426		
	Total	103	3.17	0.673	Total	46.247	102			

Table(22) shows that there were statistically significant differences in the degree of organizational justice and its role in achieving institutional excellence from the point of view of workers in the directorates of education in Hebron due to the variable of years of service. where the statistical significance< 0.05 is statistically significant. The researcher attributed this to the fact that the more the service of the employee increased his functional needs and increased ambitions and thus changed his view of the concept of organizational justice. To find out the source of the differences, the LSD test is extracted as in Table (23):

Table (23): LSD test to show the differences in the degree of organizational justice and its role in achieving institutional excellence in the directorates of education in Hebron from the point of view of its employees according to the years of service.

Years of service	Less than 5	5-less than 10	10-less than 15	15 years and above
Less than 5	–	*0.73840	–	–
5-less than 10	–*0.73840	–	–	–
10-less than 15	–	–	–	–
15 years and above	–	–	–	–

Table (23) shows that there are differences between workers in the directorates of education in Hebron who served (less than 5 years) and those who served (from 5 to less than 10 years) In favor of their service (less than 5 years)) with a difference of (0.73840).

Table (24): The arithmetical averages, standard deviations, test results and the results of the analysis of the single variance analysis to indicate the differences in the degree of organizational justice and its role in achieving the institutional excellence in the directorates of education in Hebron from the point of view of its employees according to the variable: Directorate.

Fields	Directorate	NO	Mean	Std. Deviation	Source of variance	Sum of squares	df	Mean square	F	Sig
Organizational justice and achieving institutional excellence	North Hebron	24	3.13	0.660	Between groups	0.895	3	0.298	0.651	0.584
	Hebron	23	3.08	0.669						
	South Hebron	30	3.12	0.750	Within groups	45.392	99	0.458		
	Yatta	26	3.33	0.604						
	Total	103	3.17	0.673	Total	46.247	102			

Table (24) shows that there were no statistically significant differences in the degree of organizational justice and its role in achieving institutional excellence from the point of view of workers in the directorates of education in Hebron due to the variable of the directorate. where the statistical significance> 0.05 is not statistically significant. The researcher attributed the reason to the fact that the sense of organizational justice and the availability of functional stability of the workers is not related to the workplace, since all districts are similar in the prevailing leadership styles and in the surrounding environmental conditions because the source of instructions, laws and incentives is the Ministry of Education and Higher Education.

*There is no statistically significant relationship at the level of significance($\alpha \leq 0.05$)in the degree of organizational justice and achievement of institutional excellence in the directorates of education in Hebron from the point of view of its employees.

Table (25):Pearson correlation coefficient to show the relationship between organizational justice (procedural, distributive, interactive, evaluation) and its role in achieving institutional excellence in the directorates of education in Hebron (N = 113)

Variables			Person correlation	*0.627
Procedural justice	Institutional Excellence		Statistical significance	00.00
Distributive Justice	Institutional Excellence		Person correlation	*0.762
			Statistical significance	00.00
Interactive Justice	Institutional Excellence		Person correlation	*0.724
			Statistical significance	00.00
Evaluation Justice	Institutional Excellence		Person correlation	*0.705
			Statistical significance	00.00
Organizational justice in general	Institutional Excellence		Person correlation	*0.788
			Statistical significance	00.00

Table (25) shows statistically significant correlation at the level of significance ($\alpha \leq$ 0.05) between organizational justice in all its fields (procedural justice, distributive justice, interactive justice, evaluative justice) and institutional excellence from the point of view of workers in the directorates of education in Hebron governorate.

*There are no statistically significant differences at the level of significance ($\alpha \leq 0.05$) in the degree of the practice of transformational management and its role in achieving institutional excellence from the point of view of its employees in Hebron according to the variables: (gender, Age, scientific qualification, job title, years of service, Directorate). To answer this hypothesis, the arithmetical averages and standard deviations, the results of the T- test, and the results of the single-variance analysis test were extracted. This is shown in Tables 26-31.

Table (26): The results of the "T" test indicate the differences in the practice of transformational management and the achievement of institutional excellence according to the variable: gender.

Variables	Gender	Number	Mean	Std Deviation	df	T value	Sig (2-tailed
The practice of transformational management and achieving institutional excellence	Male	72	3.21	0.699	71	2.447	0.016
	Female	31	2.85	0.646	30		

Function at the level of significance($\alpha \leq 0.05$)

Table (26) showed that there were statistically significant differences in the practice of transformational management and its role in achieving the institutional excellence due to the gender variable. The statistical significance was< 0.05 which is statistically significant. The differences were in favor of males. The researcher attributed this to the increase in the number of males in the study sample compared to the number of females.

Table (27): The mean and standard deviations, the results of the test and the results of the test of the analysis of the single variance to indicate the differences in the degree of transformational management and its role in achieving the institutional excellence in the directorates of education in Hebron from the point of view of its employees according to the variable: Age.

Fields	Age	NO	Mean	Std. Deviation	Source of variance	Sum of squares	df	Mean square	F	Sig
The practice of transformational management and achieving institutional excellence	Less than 30	8	3.21	1.08	Between groups	1.096	3	0.365	0.739	0.532
	From 30 to less than 40	40	2.98	0.746						
	From 40- to less than 50	37	3.21	0.614						
	50 years and over	18	3.11	0.560	Within groups	48.955	99	0.499		
	Total	103	3.11	0.700	Total	50.051	102			

34

Table (27) shows that the results of the study showed that there were no statistically significant differences in the degree of the practice of transformational management and its role in achieving the institutional excellence due to the variable of age, where the statistical significance was > 0.05 which is not statistically significant. Subject to the same laws, regulations and instructions regardless of age.

Table (28): The mean and standard deviations, the results of the test and the results of the test of the analysis of the single variance to indicate the differences in the degree of transformational management and its role in achieving the institutional excellence in the directorates of education in Hebron from the point of view of its employees according to the variable: qualification .

Fields	qualific ation	NO	Mean	Std. Deviation	Source of variance	Sum of squares	df	Mean square	F	Sig
The practice of transformational management and achieving institutional excellence	Diploma and less	9	3.18	0.826	Between groups	0.162	2	0.081	0.16 2	0.850
	BA	73	3.12	0.674	Within groups	49.889	100	0.499		
	Master and above	21	3.04	0.764						
	Total	103	3.11	0.700	Total	50.051	102			

Table (28) shows that the results of the study showed that there were no statistically significant differences in the practice of transformational management and its role in achieving the institutional excellence due to the variable of scientific qualification, where the statistical significance was > 0.05 which is not statistically significant. Subject to the same laws, regulations and instructions regardless of their scientific qualifications.

Table (29): The mean and standard deviations, the results of the test and the results of the test of the analysis of the single variance to indicate the differences in the degree of transformational management and its role in achieving the institutional excellence in the directorates of education in Hebron from the point of view of its employees according to the variable:: Job title.

Fields	Job title	NO	Mean	Std. Deviation	Source of variance	Sum of squares	df	Mean square	F	Sig
The practice of transformational management and achieving institutional excellence	administrative employee	43	3.24	0.747	Between groups	0.160	2	0.286	0.626	0.545
	Educational Supervisor	31	3.06	0.545	Within groups	49.891	100	0.457		
	Head of the Department	29	3.18	0.689						
	Total	103	3.17	0.673	Total	50.051	102			

Table (29) shows that the results of the study showed that there were no statistically significant differences in the practice of transformational management and its role in achieving the institutional excellence due to the variable of job title. where the statistical significance> 0.05 is not statistically significant. The researcher attributes the result to central decision-making, and the inability of managers to effectively transformational management.

36

Table (30): The mean and standard deviations, the results of the test and the results of the test of the analysis of the single variance to indicate the differences in the degree of transformational management and its role in achieving the institutional excellence in the directorates of education in Hebron from the point of view of its employees according to the variable: years of service.

Fields	Years of service	NO	Mean	Std. Deviation	Source of variance	Sum of squares	df	Mean square	F	Sig
The practice of transformational management and achieving institutional excellence	Less than 5 years	10	3.42	0.595	Between groups	3.209	3	1.070	2.260	0.086
	From 5 - less than 10 years	25	2.83	0.785						
	from 10 - less than 15 years	19	3.13	0.749	Within groups	46.842	99	0.473		
	15 years and above	49	3.18	0.624						
	Total	103	3.11	0.700	Total	50.051	102			

Table (30) shows that the results of the study showed that there were no statistically significant differences in the degree of the practice of transformational management and its role in achieving the institutional excellence due to variable years of service, where statistical significance was>0.05 which is not statistically significant. Employees are subject to the same rules, regulations and instructions regardless of their years of service.

Table (31): The mean and standard deviations, the results of the test and the results of the test of the analysis of the single variance to indicate the differences in the degree of transformational management and its role in achieving the institutional excellence in the directorates of education in Hebron from the point of view of its employees according to the variable: Directorate.

Fields	Directorate	NO	Mean	Std. Deviation	Source of variance	Sum of squares	df	Mean square	F	Sig
The practice of transformational management and achieving institutional excellence	North Hebron	24	3.16	0.642	Between groups	1.463	3	0.488	0.994	0.399
	Hebron	23	2.94	0.673						
	South Hebron	30	3.05	0.735	Within groups	48.588	99	0.491		
	Yatta	26	3.27	0.732						
	Total	103	3.11	0.700	Total	50.051	102			

Table (31) shows that the results of the study showed that there were no statistically significant differences in the degree of practice of the transformational management and its role in achieving the institutional excellence due to the variable of the directorate, where the statistical significance was >0.05 which is not statistically significant. Are subject to the same regulations, laws and instructions in all districts in Hebron Governorate, where the source of the instructions is one of the Ministry of Education and Higher Education.

*There is no statistically significant relationship at the level of significance ($\alpha \leq 0.05$) in the degree of practicing transformational management and achieving institutional excellence in the directorates of education in Hebron from the point of view of its employees.

Table (32):Pearson correlation coefficient to show the relationship between transformational management and its role in achieving institutional excellence in the directorates of education in Hebron (N = 113)

Variables			Person correlation	**0.651
The ideal effect	Institutional Excellence		Statistical significance	00.00
Inspirational stimulation	Institutional Excellence		Person correlation	**0.762
			Statistical significance	00.00
Thought provoking	Institutional Excellence		Person correlation	*0.714
			Statistical significance	00.00
Individual consideration	Institutional Excellence		Person correlation	*0.720
			Statistical significance	00.00
Transformational management in general	Institutional Excellence		Person correlation	*0.792
			Statistical significance	00.00

Function at the level of significance(α≤0.05)

Table (32): shows statistically significant correlation at the level of significance ($\alpha \leq$ 0.05) between the practice of transformational management and the achievement of institutional excellence in the overall degree, and in all areas of transformational management (ideal effect, inspirational stimulation, thought provoking, individual consideration) The statistical significance is <0.05, so we reject the null hypothesis and accept the alternative hypothesis which states that there is a statistically significant relationship at the level of significance ($\alpha \leq$ 0.05) in the practice of transformational management and its role in achieving institutional excellence.

Summary of the main results:
 In light of the analysis of the data, the study reached the following results:
-The level of organizational justice in the directorates of education in Hebron from the point of view of its employees is generally medium. The highest fields is organizational justice, followed by distributive justice, followed by evaluation justice, Finally Procedural justice.
-The level of procedural justice in the directorates of education in Hebron from the point of view of its employees is medium. The paragraph "I feel that my duties and duties are appropriate" is high, while the paragraph "I think the financial incentives offered to me is appropriate" is low.
-The level of distributive justice in the directorates of education in Hebron is medium - The paragraph "The official responsible gives the employees the right to leave ", and the paragraph" the official grants part of his powers to the workers according to his specialties " is high, while The paragraph "I feel that the civil service law gives me appropriate incentives" is low.
-The level of interactive justice in the directorates of education in Hebron from the point of view of its employees is medium. The paragraph " Delegation of some administrative responsibilities to some members ", while all other paragraphs were medium.
-The level of evaluation justice in the directorates of education in Hebron from the point of view of its employees is medium. The paragraph "I have the opportunity to object to a performance evaluation if I feel unfair " and a paragraph " I have knowledge of the criteria by which my performance is assessed" is high, while the paragraph "the official is keen to reward outstanding employees for Performance " is low .
-The level of institutional excellence in the directorates of education in Hebron from the point of view of its employees is generally medium. The highest field of institutional excellence is Leadership excellence, followed by the field of excellence in service delivery, and finally the field of human excellence.
-The level of leadership excellence in the directorates of education in Hebron from the point of view of its employees is medium. The paragraph "The management of the directorate continuously seeks excellence in providing service to the public" is high , Otherwise all paragraphs is medium.
-The level of human excellence in the directorates of education in Hebron from the point of view of its employees is medium. The paragraph "Employees receive rewards commensurate with their assessment " , and the paragraph "The Directorate offers the opportunity to send distinguished employees" is low, while the rest of the paragraphs to a medium degree.
-The level of excellence in providing service in the directorates of education in Hebron from the point of view of its employees is medium . while the rest of all paragraphs to a medium degree.
-There were statistically significant differences in the degree of organizational justice and its role in achieving institutional excellence from the point of view of workers in the

directorates of education in Hebron due to the gender variable. The statistical significance is < 0.05, which is a statistical function, The differences were in favor of males.

-The results of the study showed that there were no statistically significant differences in the degree of organizational justice and its role in achieving institutional excellence from the point of view of workers in the directorates of education in Hebron due to the variables: (age, academic qualification, job title, directorate), Where the statistical significance> 0.05 is not statistically significant.

-The results showed there were statistically significant differences in the degree of organizational justice and its role in achieving institutional excellence from the point of view of workers in the directorates of education in Hebron due to the variables:(gender, of years of service). where the statistical significance< 0.05 is statistically significant. The differences between workers in the directorates of education in Hebron who served (less than 5 years) and those who served (from 5 to less than 10 years) In favor of their service (less than 5 years)) with a difference of (0.73840).

-The study shows statistically significant correlation at the level of significance ($\alpha \leq$ 0.05) between organizational justice in all its fields (procedural justice, distributive justice, interactive justice, evaluative justice) and institutional excellence from the point of view of workers in the directorates of education in Hebron governorate.

-The degree of the practice of transformational management from the point of view of workers in the directorates of education in Hebron governorate from the point of view of the subordinates was medium on the total degree and in all its fields (ideal effect, inspirational motivation, thought provoking, individual consideration).

-The highest areas of the practice of transformational management were the field of thought-provoking, followed by the field of inspirational motivation, followed by the ideal influence and finally the area of individual interest.

-The results show that the official is interested in giving incentives to make the change, and it gives meaning to work by motivating and encouraging the employees, and also takes into account the individual differences between workers in the area of needs and desires, and maintains communication and communication with employees in different opinions and affiliations, The development of work courageously, gives time to listen to the ideas of workers, and works to stimulate thinking to solve problems.

-While the results showed that the official deals unsatisfactorily with the employees, it does not raise the challenge and stability in the workers, and does not trust everyone in large extent, does not proceed the process of delegation of work, to check on the progress of work and success.

-The degree of institutional excellence in the directorates of education in the governorate of Hebron from the point of view of the employees was medium on the overall score, and that the highest areas of excellence were leadership excellence, followed by excellence in service delivery, and finally human excellence.

-It turns out that the management of the institution constantly seeks to excellence in providing service to the public.

-Employees are found to have no rewards for their assessment, and the Foundation does not provide opportunities for the recruitment of outstanding staff.

-The results of the study showed that there are no statistically significant differences in the degree of practice of transformational management and its role in achieving institutional excellence from the point of view of workers in the directorates of education in Hebron governorate due to the variables: the scientific qualification, age, years of service and administration. While differences were found to be statistically significant by gender variable and the differences were in favor of males.

-There is a statistically significant correlation between the practice of transformational management and the achievement of institutional excellence from the point of view of workers in the directorates of education in Hebron governorate on the overall degree, and in all areas of transformational management (ideal effect, inspirational motivation, thought provoking, individual consideration).

Study Recommendations:

In light of the results and objectives of the study, the researcher recommends the following:

1.The Palestinian Ministry of Education and Higher Education should amend the prevailing procedures and laws in order to raise the level of organizational justice because of its active role in achieving institutional excellence.

2. Work on the development of an effective system of incentives and granting appropriate financial incentives for workers to achieve the desired institutional excellence.

3. Amend the civil service law to suit the needs of employees and achieve the public interest.

4. The need to reward outstanding employees in performance (positive motivation).

5.Holding training courses for employees and informing them of the latest developments in the field of administrative sciences and the mechanism of achieving competitive advantage in the institution, and work to send distinguished employees.

6. The Ministry of Education should reduce the centralization of the work.

7.Work to improve the functional conditions of administrative staff.

8.Non-concentration of powers in the hands of the official and encourage the delegation of powers to subordinates.

9. Urge officials to deal satisfactorily with employees.

10. Urge officials to raise the challenge and consistency of employees.

11. The need to provide an atmosphere of trust and security between the president and the subordinate.

12. Provide rewards for employees to suit their evaluation.

13. Providing scholarships for distinguished employees.

References:

-Abu Haddaf, S. (2011), The role of transformational management in the development of the effectiveness of teaching teachers in UNRWA schools in Gaza, *(Unpublished Master Thesis)*, Al-Azhar University, Gaza, Palestine.

-Adam. G. Otaibi,.(2003). "The influence of Organizational Justice on Employee Attitudes in Public Organizational State of Kuwait ", *Journal of Administrative Science* , University of Kuwait , Vol.(10), No.(3) , p.p. 343-362.

-Adams, J. S. (1965). "Towards an Understanding of Inequity" *Journal of Abnormal and Social Psychology*, 67, 422-436.

-Ahamdi, F, & Tavreh, N.(2011). " Survey Relationship between Organizational Justice and Organizational Citizenship Behavior (OCB) Of Food Product Firms in Kurdestan Province, Interdisciplinary, *Journal of Contemporary Research in Business,* vol.(2), No.(10), P.P. 272-281.

-Ameri, A. (2001), Transformational Leadership Behavior and Organizational Citizenship Behavior in Saudi Government Agencies, *Arab Journal of Administrative Sciences*, 9(1), 19-39.

-Awad, A. (2003). "Analyzing the Dimensions of Organizational Justice": Applied Study, Cairo, Ain Shams University, Faculty of Commerce, *Journal of Administrative Research*, January 2003, p.

-Barakat, Z. (2014). "The Degree of Organizational Justice among Principals of Public Schools in Palestine from the Point of View of their School Teachers", *Journal of Psychological and Educational Studies*", Vol. 10, No. 1, January 2016, Muscat, Sultanate of Oman.

-Beardwell, L, & Holden, L. (2001). **Human Resource Management:** Contemporary approach, 3rd (Ed), England, Financial Times, Prentice hall.

-Borghini ,E,C.(2013). "Framework for the study of relationships between organizational characteristics and organizational innovation **"** *the journal of creative Behavior* ,vol ,(31),No ,(1) :226-289 .

-Buhaisi, A. (2014). "The Role of Empowering Employees in Achieving Institutional Excellence - A Field Study on Technical Colleges in the Governorates of the Gaza Strip" *(unpublished Master Thesis)*, Deanship of Graduate Studies, Al-Azhar University, Gaza, Palestine.

- Burns, J. (1978), Leadership, NY; Harder & Row.

-Che-Meh, S. & Nasurdin, M. (2009), The Relationships Between Job Resources, Job Demands and Teachers' OCB. Retrieved November 15, 2009, from www.usm.my.

-Daft,R.(2000)."**Management"** ,The Dryden press, New York.P22.

-Edralin, Divina M, (2010), "Human Resource Management Practices: Drivers for Stimulating Corporate Entrepreneurship in Large Companies in the Philippines" *DLSU Business & Economics Review*, Vol.(19), No.(2): 25-41.

-Ghamdi, S. (2000), Transformational Management in Saudi Universities, Extent of Practice and Characteristics of Academic Leaders,*(unpublished PhD thesis)*, Umm Al-Qura University, Saudi Arabia.

-Ghazi, A. (2014). "Applied Practices for the Standard of Resources and Partnerships as One of the Standards of Possibilities to Achieve Institutional Excellence", *Journal of the Successful Director, Excellence Series*, 3, pp. 8-12.

-Greenberg, d. (1990)." Organizational Justice: Yesterday, Today, and Tomorrow, *Journal of Management,* (16), 606-613.

-Hassan, A, Ahmed, H. (2010). "Human Resource Management Practices and Their Impact on Institutional Excellence - Applied Study in Zain Kuwait Mobile

Telecommunications Company", *(Unpublished Master Thesis)*, Middle East University.

-Hawari, S. (1996), **"The features of the future director from mutual leadership to transformational management"**, Ein Shams Library, Cairo, Egypt.

-Hilali & Hilali. (2001), The Use of Theory of Transformational Management and Procedural Leadership in Some Academic Faculties (Analytical Study), *Journal of the Future of Arab Education*, Cairo, 7(21), 95-120.

-Idris, W; & Zahir M. (2009). **"Strategic Performance Management: Fundamentals of Performance and Balanced Scorecard"**, Amman, Jordan: Dar Wael Publishing and Distribution.

-Kim, J, (2010), "Strategic Human Resource Practices: Introducing Alternatives for Organizational Performance Improvement in the Public Sector", *Public Administration Review*, January – February: 38-49.

-Miles ,A.J.," The cumulative Effects of Justice Perceptions", *The Journal of Applied Management*, Vol.(2),No(1),2000 ,p.12.

-Musa, P, Tulay, G, (2008), "Investigating the Impact of Organizational Excellence and Leadership on Business Performance: An Exploratory Study of Turkish Firms", *SAM Advanced Management Journal*, Vol.(73), No.(1): 29-45.

-Niehoff, B; Moorman, R. (1993). "Justice As a Mediator of The Relationship Between Methods of Monitoring And Organizational Citizenship Behavior". *Academy of management Journal*, Vol. 35 (3), 527-556.

-Nuaimi, A; & Rabat J. (2008). **"Achieving Accuracy in Quality Management: Concepts and Practices"**, Amman, Jordan: Dar Al Yazuri Publishing and Distribution.

-Otaibi, S.(2005), **"The Role of Transformational Management" in Change Management, Research presented to the Third Management Forum"**, Development Management and Development Requirements in Administrative Work (Towards Effective Change Management), Jeddah, Saudi Arabia.

-Owens, R. (1995), **"Organizational Behavior in Education wren"**, Thomas the Leaders companion, New York: The Free Press .

-Rokab, A.(2010), The Relationship of Transformational Management to the Empowerment of Workers in Palestinian Universities in Gaza , *(Unpublished Master Thesis)*, Al-Azhar University, Gaza, Palestine.

-Selmi, A. (2001). **"Thoughts on Contemporary Management"**, Cairo, Egypt: Dar Ghareeb for Publishing and Distribution.

-Soud , R; & Sultan, S. (2009). "The Degree of Organizational Justice in the Heads of Academic Departments in the Official Jordanian Universities and their Relation to the Organizational Loyalty of Faculty Members", *Damascus University Journal*, Vol. 25, No. 1 + 2, Damascus.

-Twail, H. (1999),Transformational Management Concepts and Horizons, Amman: Dar Wael Publishing and Distribution.

-Yilmaz, K,. (2010), "Teachers Perceptions about Organizational Public School Secondary Justice.", *Practice and Educational Science Journal*, Vol.(10), No.(1): 603-616.

-Zayed, A. (2003). "Outstanding Organizational Performance: The Way to Future Organization": *Arab Organization for Administrative Development*, Cairo.

-Ziad, A. (2006). "Organizational Justice": *The Next Task for Human Resource Management: Arab Organization for Administrative Development,* Cairo, p. 12.

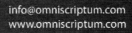

Printed by Books on Demand GmbH, Norderstedt / Germany